50 Wedding Reception Recipes for Home

By: Kelly Johnson

Table of Contents

- Mini Beef Wellingtons
- Stuffed Mushrooms with Cream Cheese and Garlic
- Caprese Skewers with Balsamic Glaze
- Bacon-Wrapped Dates Stuffed with Goat Cheese
- Shrimp Cocktail with Cocktail Sauce
- Chicken Satay with Peanut Dipping Sauce
- Spinach and Artichoke Dip with Tortilla Chips
- Bruschetta with Tomato and Basil
- Mini Crab Cakes with Remoulade Sauce
- Vegetable Spring Rolls with Sweet Chili Sauce
- Teriyaki Meatballs
- Prosciutto-Wrapped Melon
- Deviled Eggs with Smoked Salmon
- Mediterranean Hummus Platter with Pita Bread
- Assorted Cheese and Crackers Platter
- Smoked Salmon Crostini with Dill Cream Cheese
- Grilled Vegetable Platter with Herb Dip
- Chicken Quesadillas with Salsa and Guacamole
- Antipasto Skewers with Salami, Olives, and Mozzarella
- Mini Quiches with Various Fillings (e.g., spinach, bacon, cheese)
- Coconut Shrimp with Mango Dipping Sauce
- Brie and Raspberry Phyllo Cups
- Cucumber Cups with Herbed Cream Cheese
- Teriyaki Glazed Salmon Skewers
- Assorted Sushi Rolls
- Meat and Cheese Charcuterie Board
- Crab Stuffed Mushrooms
- Spanakopita Triangles (Spinach and Feta in Filo Pastry)
- Chicken and Waffle Sliders with Maple Syrup
- Tuna Tartare on Wonton Crisps
- Bacon-Wrapped Scallops
- Assorted Bruschetta Trio (Tomato Basil, Olive Tapenade, Fig and Prosciutto)
- Mini Lobster Rolls
- Gourmet Macaroni and Cheese Bites

- Chicken Caesar Salad Bites in Parmesan Cups
- Beef Sliders with Caramelized Onions and Gruyère Cheese
- Mushroom Risotto Balls
- Stuffed Jalapeño Poppers with Cream Cheese and Bacon
- Mini Croque Monsieur Bites
- Falafel Balls with Tzatziki Sauce
- Peking Duck Pancakes with Hoisin Sauce
- Smoked Trout Pâté on Crostini
- Miniature Beef Tacos with Guacamole and Salsa
- Buffalo Chicken Meatballs with Blue Cheese Dip
- Teriyaki Tofu Skewers
- Fig and Goat Cheese Crostini with Honey Drizzle
- Crab Rangoon with Sweet and Sour Sauce
- Miniature Beef Wellingtons
- Bacon-Wrapped Jalapeño Poppers Stuffed with Cream Cheese
- Spinach and Feta Spanakopita Triangles

Mini Beef Wellingtons

Ingredients:

- 1 lb beef tenderloin fillet, cut into 1-inch cubes
- Salt and pepper to taste
- Olive oil
- 2 tablespoons butter
- 1 small onion, finely chopped
- 2 cloves garlic, minced
- 8 oz mushrooms, finely chopped
- 2 tablespoons chopped fresh parsley
- 1 sheet puff pastry, thawed
- 1 egg, beaten (for egg wash)

Instructions:

1. Season the beef cubes with salt and pepper.
2. Heat a skillet over medium-high heat and add a drizzle of olive oil. Sear the beef cubes on all sides until browned, about 1-2 minutes per side. Remove from the skillet and set aside.
3. In the same skillet, melt the butter over medium heat. Add the chopped onion and cook until softened, about 2-3 minutes. Add the minced garlic and cook for another 1 minute.
4. Add the finely chopped mushrooms to the skillet and cook until they release their moisture and become golden brown, about 5-7 minutes. Stir in the chopped parsley and season with salt and pepper to taste. Remove from heat and let cool slightly.
5. Preheat the oven to 400°F (200°C).
6. Roll out the thawed puff pastry on a lightly floured surface. Cut the pastry into squares large enough to wrap around each beef cube.
7. Place a spoonful of the mushroom mixture in the center of each pastry square. Top with a seared beef cube.
8. Fold the pastry over the beef and mushroom filling, sealing the edges tightly. Place the wrapped mini Beef Wellingtons seam side down on a baking sheet lined with parchment paper.

9. Brush the tops of the mini Beef Wellingtons with beaten egg to create a golden brown finish when baked.
10. Bake in the preheated oven for 15-20 minutes, or until the pastry is puffed and golden brown.
11. Remove from the oven and let cool slightly before serving.
12. Serve the mini Beef Wellingtons warm as a delicious appetizer at your wedding reception.

These mini Beef Wellingtons are sure to impress your guests with their tender beef, savory mushroom filling, and flaky puff pastry crust. Enjoy!

Stuffed Mushrooms with Cream Cheese and Garlic

Ingredients:

- 24 large mushrooms, cleaned with stems removed
- 8 oz cream cheese, softened
- 2 cloves garlic, minced
- 1/4 cup grated Parmesan cheese
- 2 tablespoons chopped fresh parsley
- Salt and pepper to taste
- Olive oil or melted butter for brushing
- Optional: breadcrumbs for topping

Instructions:

1. Preheat your oven to 375°F (190°C). Line a baking sheet with parchment paper or lightly grease it with olive oil.
2. In a mixing bowl, combine the softened cream cheese, minced garlic, grated Parmesan cheese, chopped parsley, salt, and pepper. Mix well until all ingredients are thoroughly combined.
3. Spoon the cream cheese mixture into each mushroom cap, filling them generously. If desired, sprinkle breadcrumbs on top for added texture.
4. Place the stuffed mushrooms on the prepared baking sheet, evenly spaced apart.
5. Brush the tops of the stuffed mushrooms with olive oil or melted butter to help them brown nicely in the oven.
6. Bake in the preheated oven for 20-25 minutes, or until the mushrooms are tender and the filling is golden and bubbly.
7. Once done, remove the stuffed mushrooms from the oven and let them cool slightly before serving.
8. Arrange the stuffed mushrooms on a serving platter and garnish with additional chopped parsley if desired.
9. Serve the stuffed mushrooms warm as a delicious appetizer at your wedding reception.

These stuffed mushrooms are sure to be a hit with your guests, with their creamy and flavorful filling and tender mushroom caps. Enjoy!

Caprese Skewers with Balsamic Glaze

Ingredients:

- Cherry or grape tomatoes
- Fresh mozzarella balls (bocconcini)
- Fresh basil leaves
- Balsamic glaze (store-bought or homemade)
- Wooden skewers

Instructions:

1. Rinse the cherry or grape tomatoes and pat them dry with paper towels. Similarly, drain any excess liquid from the fresh mozzarella balls.
2. To assemble the skewers, thread one cherry tomato, one mozzarella ball, and one basil leaf onto each wooden skewer. Repeat this process until all skewers are assembled.
3. Arrange the assembled skewers on a serving platter or tray.
4. Just before serving, drizzle the skewers with balsamic glaze. You can either use store-bought balsamic glaze or make your own by reducing balsamic vinegar over low heat until it thickens into a syrupy consistency.
5. If desired, you can also sprinkle some freshly ground black pepper or sea salt over the skewers for added flavor.
6. Serve the Caprese skewers with balsamic glaze immediately as a delightful appetizer at your wedding reception.

These Caprese skewers are not only visually appealing but also bursting with fresh flavors from the tomatoes, mozzarella, basil, and balsamic glaze. They're sure to be a hit with your guests! Enjoy!

Bacon-Wrapped Dates Stuffed with Goat Cheese

Ingredients:

- Medjool dates, pitted (about 24)
- Goat cheese (about 4 ounces)
- Bacon slices (12 slices, cut in half)
- Toothpicks or cocktail sticks

Instructions:

1. Preheat your oven to 375°F (190°C). Line a baking sheet with parchment paper or aluminum foil for easy cleanup.
2. Slice each date lengthwise on one side to create an opening. Remove the pits if they're not already pitted.
3. Fill each date with a small amount of goat cheese, using a spoon or your fingers to press it into the cavity.
4. Wrap each stuffed date with a half-slice of bacon, securing it with a toothpick or cocktail stick.
5. Place the bacon-wrapped dates on the prepared baking sheet, spacing them out evenly.
6. Bake in the preheated oven for 15-20 minutes, or until the bacon is crispy and cooked to your liking.
7. Once done, remove the bacon-wrapped dates from the oven and let them cool slightly before serving.
8. Serve the bacon-wrapped dates stuffed with goat cheese warm as a delicious appetizer at your wedding reception.

These bacon-wrapped dates are the perfect combination of sweet, salty, and creamy, making them a crowd-pleasing appetizer option for any occasion. Enjoy!

Shrimp Cocktail with Cocktail Sauce

Ingredients:

For the shrimp:

- 1 lb large shrimp, peeled and deveined (tails on or off, depending on preference)
- Salt
- Lemon wedges, for serving

For the cocktail sauce:

- 1 cup ketchup
- 2 tablespoons prepared horseradish (adjust to taste)
- 1 tablespoon fresh lemon juice
- 1 teaspoon Worcestershire sauce
- Dash of hot sauce (optional)
- Salt and pepper to taste

Instructions:

1. Bring a large pot of salted water to a boil. Add the shrimp and cook until they turn pink and opaque, about 2-3 minutes. Be careful not to overcook. Drain the shrimp and transfer them to a bowl of ice water to stop the cooking process. Once cooled, drain again and pat dry with paper towels.
2. In a small bowl, mix together the ketchup, prepared horseradish, lemon juice, Worcestershire sauce, hot sauce (if using), salt, and pepper to make the cocktail sauce. Adjust the seasoning to taste. Cover and refrigerate until ready to serve.
3. Arrange the cooked shrimp on a serving platter or individual cocktail glasses.
4. Serve the shrimp cocktail with the chilled cocktail sauce and lemon wedges on the side.
5. Optionally, garnish the platter with fresh parsley or lettuce leaves for presentation.
6. Serve immediately and enjoy this classic appetizer at your wedding reception.

Shrimp cocktail is a timeless appetizer that's sure to impress your guests with its simplicity and flavor. Enjoy!

Chicken Satay with Peanut Dipping Sauce

Ingredients:

For the chicken satay:

- 1 lb boneless, skinless chicken breasts or thighs, cut into thin strips
- 1/4 cup soy sauce
- 2 tablespoons brown sugar
- 2 cloves garlic, minced
- 1 tablespoon grated fresh ginger
- 1 teaspoon ground coriander
- 1/2 teaspoon ground turmeric
- 1/4 teaspoon ground cumin
- Bamboo skewers, soaked in water for 30 minutes

For the peanut dipping sauce:

- 1/2 cup creamy peanut butter
- 1/4 cup coconut milk
- 2 tablespoons soy sauce
- 1 tablespoon brown sugar
- 1 tablespoon lime juice
- 1 clove garlic, minced
- 1 teaspoon grated fresh ginger
- 1/4 teaspoon red pepper flakes (optional)
- Water (to adjust consistency)

Instructions:

1. In a bowl, combine the soy sauce, brown sugar, minced garlic, grated ginger, ground coriander, ground turmeric, and ground cumin. Add the chicken strips and toss until they are well coated. Cover and marinate in the refrigerator for at least 1 hour, or overnight for best flavor.
2. While the chicken is marinating, prepare the peanut dipping sauce. In a small saucepan over medium heat, combine the peanut butter, coconut milk, soy sauce, brown sugar, lime juice, minced garlic, grated ginger, and red pepper flakes (if using). Cook, stirring constantly, until the sauce is smooth and well combined. If

the sauce is too thick, you can thin it out with a little water until you reach your desired consistency. Remove from heat and set aside.
3. Preheat your grill or grill pan over medium-high heat. Thread the marinated chicken strips onto the soaked bamboo skewers.
4. Grill the chicken satay skewers for 3-4 minutes on each side, or until they are cooked through and have nice grill marks.
5. Transfer the grilled chicken satay skewers to a serving platter and serve them warm with the peanut dipping sauce on the side.
6. Optionally, garnish with chopped cilantro and crushed peanuts for extra flavor and texture.

Enjoy your delicious chicken satay with peanut dipping sauce at your wedding reception!

Spinach and Artichoke Dip with Tortilla Chips

Ingredients:

For the spinach and artichoke dip:

- 1 (10 oz) package frozen chopped spinach, thawed and drained
- 1 (14 oz) can artichoke hearts, drained and chopped
- 8 oz cream cheese, softened
- 1/2 cup sour cream
- 1/2 cup mayonnaise
- 1 cup shredded mozzarella cheese
- 1/2 cup grated Parmesan cheese
- 2 cloves garlic, minced
- 1/2 teaspoon onion powder
- 1/2 teaspoon dried basil
- 1/2 teaspoon dried oregano
- Salt and pepper to taste

For serving:

- Tortilla chips

Instructions:

1. Preheat your oven to 375°F (190°C).
2. In a large mixing bowl, combine the thawed and drained chopped spinach, chopped artichoke hearts, softened cream cheese, sour cream, mayonnaise, shredded mozzarella cheese, grated Parmesan cheese, minced garlic, onion powder, dried basil, dried oregano, salt, and pepper. Mix until well combined.
3. Transfer the spinach and artichoke dip mixture to a greased baking dish, spreading it out evenly.
4. Bake in the preheated oven for 25-30 minutes, or until the dip is hot and bubbly, and the top is golden brown.
5. Remove the dip from the oven and let it cool for a few minutes before serving.
6. Serve the spinach and artichoke dip warm with tortilla chips for dipping.

7. Optionally, you can garnish the dip with additional shredded mozzarella cheese and chopped fresh parsley before serving for extra flavor and presentation.

Enjoy this delicious spinach and artichoke dip with tortilla chips at your wedding reception! It's creamy, cheesy, and packed with flavor, making it the perfect crowd-pleasing appetizer.

Bruschetta with Tomato and Basil

Ingredients:

- 4-5 ripe tomatoes, diced
- 1/4 cup fresh basil leaves, chopped
- 2 cloves garlic, minced
- 2 tablespoons extra virgin olive oil
- 1 tablespoon balsamic vinegar
- Salt and pepper to taste
- Baguette or Italian bread, sliced

Instructions:

1. In a mixing bowl, combine the diced tomatoes, chopped basil leaves, minced garlic, extra virgin olive oil, and balsamic vinegar. Season with salt and pepper to taste. Stir gently to combine all the ingredients.
2. Let the tomato mixture sit at room temperature for about 15-20 minutes to allow the flavors to meld together.
3. Preheat your oven broiler or grill to medium-high heat.
4. Arrange the sliced baguette or Italian bread on a baking sheet in a single layer.
5. Brush each slice of bread lightly with olive oil on both sides.
6. Place the baking sheet under the preheated broiler or on the grill and cook the bread slices for 1-2 minutes on each side, or until they are lightly toasted and golden brown.
7. Remove the toasted bread slices from the oven or grill and let them cool slightly.
8. Once cooled, spoon the tomato and basil mixture generously onto each toasted bread slice.
9. Arrange the bruschetta on a serving platter and garnish with additional basil leaves, if desired.
10. Serve the bruschetta with tomato and basil immediately as a delicious appetizer at your wedding reception.

This bruschetta with tomato and basil is fresh, flavorful, and sure to impress your guests with its simplicity and taste. Enjoy!

Mini Crab Cakes with Remoulade Sauce

Ingredients:

For the crab cakes:

- 1 lb lump crabmeat, picked over for shells
- 1/2 cup mayonnaise
- 1/4 cup finely chopped green onions
- 1/4 cup finely chopped red bell pepper
- 1/4 cup finely chopped celery
- 1 large egg
- 1 tablespoon Dijon mustard
- 1 tablespoon Worcestershire sauce
- 1 tablespoon lemon juice
- 1/2 teaspoon Old Bay seasoning
- Salt and pepper to taste
- 1 cup breadcrumbs
- 2 tablespoons butter, for frying

For the remoulade sauce:

- 1/2 cup mayonnaise
- 2 tablespoons Dijon mustard
- 1 tablespoon capers, chopped
- 1 tablespoon pickle relish
- 1 tablespoon chopped fresh parsley
- 1 tablespoon lemon juice
- 1 teaspoon hot sauce (optional)
- Salt and pepper to taste

Instructions:

1. In a large mixing bowl, combine the lump crabmeat, mayonnaise, chopped green onions, chopped red bell pepper, chopped celery, egg, Dijon mustard,

Worcestershire sauce, lemon juice, Old Bay seasoning, salt, and pepper. Gently fold everything together until well combined.
2. Gradually add the breadcrumbs to the crab mixture until it holds together without being too wet. Be careful not to overmix.
3. Using your hands, shape the crab mixture into mini crab cakes, about 1 to 1.5 inches in diameter.
4. Heat the butter in a large skillet over medium heat. Once the butter is melted and hot, add the mini crab cakes in batches, making sure not to overcrowd the skillet. Cook the crab cakes for 3-4 minutes on each side, or until they are golden brown and cooked through. Transfer the cooked crab cakes to a paper towel-lined plate to drain any excess oil.
5. To make the remoulade sauce, in a small bowl, combine the mayonnaise, Dijon mustard, chopped capers, pickle relish, chopped parsley, lemon juice, hot sauce (if using), salt, and pepper. Stir until well combined. Taste and adjust seasoning if needed.
6. Serve the mini crab cakes warm with the remoulade sauce on the side for dipping.
7. Optionally, garnish the crab cakes with additional chopped parsley or a squeeze of lemon juice before serving.

Enjoy these delicious mini crab cakes with remoulade sauce as a delightful appetizer at your wedding reception!

Vegetable Spring Rolls with Sweet Chili Sauce

Ingredients:

For the vegetable spring rolls:

- 10 spring roll wrappers (8-inch size)
- 2 cups shredded cabbage
- 1 cup shredded carrots
- 1 cup bean sprouts
- 1/2 cup sliced bell peppers (any color)
- 1/2 cup sliced cucumber
- 1/4 cup chopped fresh cilantro
- 1/4 cup chopped fresh mint
- 1/4 cup chopped fresh basil
- Rice vermicelli noodles, cooked according to package instructions and cooled
- Oil for frying (optional)

For the sweet chili sauce:

- 1/2 cup sweet chili sauce
- 2 tablespoons soy sauce
- 1 tablespoon rice vinegar
- 1 tablespoon honey
- 1 teaspoon sriracha sauce (optional, for heat)

Instructions:

1. In a large bowl, combine the shredded cabbage, shredded carrots, bean sprouts, sliced bell peppers, sliced cucumber, chopped cilantro, chopped mint, and chopped basil. Toss everything together until well mixed.
2. Prepare a clean work surface and a bowl of warm water. Dip one spring roll wrapper into the warm water for a few seconds until it becomes pliable. Place the wrapper flat on the work surface.

3. Spoon a small amount of the vegetable mixture onto the bottom third of the wrapper, leaving some space on the sides. Add a small amount of cooked rice vermicelli noodles on top of the vegetables.
4. Fold the bottom of the wrapper over the filling, then fold the sides towards the center. Roll the wrapper tightly upwards to form a spring roll. Repeat with the remaining wrappers and filling.
5. If frying, heat oil in a large skillet or deep fryer to 350°F (175°C). Carefully add the spring rolls in batches and fry until golden brown and crispy, about 2-3 minutes. Remove with a slotted spoon and drain on paper towels.
6. To make the sweet chili sauce, in a small bowl, whisk together the sweet chili sauce, soy sauce, rice vinegar, honey, and sriracha sauce (if using).
7. Serve the vegetable spring rolls with the sweet chili sauce on the side for dipping.
8. Optionally, garnish the spring rolls with additional fresh herbs before serving.

Enjoy these delicious vegetable spring rolls with sweet chili sauce as a tasty appetizer at your wedding reception! They're fresh, crispy, and packed with flavor.

Teriyaki Meatballs

Ingredients:

For the meatballs:

- 1 lb ground beef or pork (or a combination)
- 1/2 cup breadcrumbs
- 1/4 cup milk
- 1 egg
- 2 cloves garlic, minced
- 1 tablespoon grated ginger
- 2 green onions, finely chopped
- Salt and pepper to taste
- 1 tablespoon vegetable oil, for cooking

For the teriyaki sauce:

- 1/2 cup soy sauce
- 1/4 cup water
- 2 tablespoons brown sugar
- 1 tablespoon honey
- 1 tablespoon rice vinegar
- 1 clove garlic, minced
- 1 teaspoon grated ginger
- 1 tablespoon cornstarch
- 2 tablespoons water

Instructions:

1. Preheat your oven to 375°F (190°C). Line a baking sheet with parchment paper or foil for easy cleanup.
2. In a large mixing bowl, combine the ground meat, breadcrumbs, milk, egg, minced garlic, grated ginger, chopped green onions, salt, and pepper. Mix until well combined.
3. Shape the meat mixture into small meatballs, about 1 inch in diameter.

4. Heat the vegetable oil in a large skillet over medium heat. Once the oil is hot, add the meatballs in batches and cook until browned on all sides, about 2-3 minutes per side. Transfer the browned meatballs to the prepared baking sheet.
5. Bake the meatballs in the preheated oven for 10-15 minutes, or until they are cooked through and no longer pink in the center.
6. While the meatballs are baking, prepare the teriyaki sauce. In a small saucepan, combine the soy sauce, water, brown sugar, honey, rice vinegar, minced garlic, and grated ginger. Bring the mixture to a simmer over medium heat.
7. In a small bowl, mix together the cornstarch and water to make a slurry. Gradually stir the slurry into the simmering sauce until it thickens to your desired consistency. Remove the sauce from heat.
8. Once the meatballs are cooked, transfer them to a serving platter and drizzle with the teriyaki sauce.
9. Optionally, garnish the teriyaki meatballs with chopped green onions or sesame seeds before serving.

Serve the teriyaki meatballs as a delicious appetizer at your wedding reception. They're savory, juicy, and packed with flavor!

Prosciutto-Wrapped Melon

Ingredients:

- 1 ripe cantaloupe or honeydew melon
- 6-8 slices of prosciutto
- Fresh basil leaves (optional, for garnish)
- Balsamic glaze (optional, for drizzling)

Instructions:

1. Slice the cantaloupe or honeydew melon in half and remove the seeds. Using a melon baller or a spoon, scoop out small balls of melon flesh and set aside.
2. Cut each slice of prosciutto in half lengthwise to create long strips.
3. Wrap each melon ball with a strip of prosciutto, securing it in place. Repeat with the remaining melon balls and prosciutto slices.
4. Arrange the prosciutto-wrapped melon balls on a serving platter.
5. If desired, garnish the platter with fresh basil leaves for an extra pop of color and flavor.
6. Optionally, drizzle balsamic glaze over the prosciutto-wrapped melon balls just before serving for a touch of sweetness and acidity.
7. Serve the prosciutto-wrapped melon as a delightful and refreshing appetizer at your wedding reception.

This appetizer is simple to prepare, yet it's sure to impress your guests with its combination of sweet melon and salty prosciutto. Enjoy!

Deviled Eggs with Smoked Salmon

Ingredients:

- 6 large eggs
- 2 oz smoked salmon, finely chopped
- 2 tablespoons mayonnaise
- 1 tablespoon Dijon mustard
- 1 tablespoon fresh dill, chopped
- 1 teaspoon lemon juice
- Salt and pepper, to taste
- Extra dill, for garnish (optional)

Instructions:

1. Hard-boil the eggs: Place the eggs in a saucepan and cover with cold water. Bring the water to a boil over medium-high heat. Once boiling, remove the saucepan from the heat, cover, and let the eggs sit in the hot water for 10-12 minutes. Then, drain the hot water and transfer the eggs to a bowl of ice water to cool for a few minutes.
2. Once the eggs are cooled, carefully peel them and cut them in half lengthwise. Remove the yolks and place them in a separate bowl. Arrange the egg white halves on a serving platter.
3. Mash the egg yolks with a fork until they are finely crumbled.
4. Add the chopped smoked salmon, mayonnaise, Dijon mustard, chopped dill, and lemon juice to the bowl with the mashed egg yolks. Mix well until all the ingredients are thoroughly combined. Season with salt and pepper to taste.
5. Spoon the smoked salmon and egg yolk mixture into the hollowed-out egg white halves, dividing it evenly among them.
6. If desired, garnish each deviled egg with a small sprig of fresh dill.
7. Chill the deviled eggs in the refrigerator for at least 30 minutes before serving to allow the flavors to meld together.
8. Serve the deviled eggs with smoked salmon as a delicious and elegant appetizer at your wedding reception.

These deviled eggs are sure to be a hit with your guests, with the combination of creamy egg yolks and smoky salmon flavors. Enjoy!

Mediterranean Hummus Platter with Pita Bread

Ingredients:

For the hummus:

- 2 cans (15 ounces each) chickpeas (garbanzo beans), drained and rinsed
- 1/4 cup tahini
- 2 cloves garlic, minced
- 1/4 cup lemon juice
- 1/4 cup extra virgin olive oil
- 1/2 teaspoon ground cumin
- Salt, to taste
- Water (optional, for desired consistency)

For the platter:

- Pita bread, cut into wedges
- Cherry tomatoes, halved
- Cucumber, sliced
- Kalamata olives
- Feta cheese, cubed or crumbled
- Red onion, thinly sliced
- Fresh parsley, chopped, for garnish
- Extra virgin olive oil, for drizzling
- Lemon wedges, for garnish (optional)

Instructions:

1. Prepare the hummus:
    - In a food processor, combine the drained and rinsed chickpeas, tahini, minced garlic, lemon juice, extra virgin olive oil, ground cumin, and salt.
    - Blend until smooth. If the hummus is too thick, you can add a little water, 1 tablespoon at a time, until you reach your desired consistency. Adjust seasoning to taste.
2. Transfer the hummus to a serving bowl or platter, spreading it out evenly.

3. Arrange the pita bread wedges, cherry tomatoes, cucumber slices, Kalamata olives, feta cheese, and thinly sliced red onion around the hummus on the platter.
4. Drizzle a little extra virgin olive oil over the hummus and garnish with chopped fresh parsley.
5. Optionally, you can add lemon wedges to the platter for guests to squeeze over the hummus before serving.
6. Serve the Mediterranean hummus platter with pita bread as an appetizer at your wedding reception.

This platter offers a beautiful presentation of vibrant colors and fresh flavors, and it's sure to be a hit with your guests. Enjoy!

Assorted Cheese and Crackers Platter

Ingredients:

For the cheese:

- Assorted cheeses such as:
    - Brie
    - Camembert
    - Cheddar
    - Gouda
    - Blue cheese
    - Goat cheese (chevre)
    - Swiss cheese
    - Havarti
    - Manchego
    - Parmesan
    - Pepper jack
    - Gruyere
    - Mozzarella (fresh or marinated)
- Total of 3-5 different types of cheese, depending on the size of your platter and preferences

For the accompaniments:

- Assorted crackers such as:
    - Water crackers
    - Wheat crackers
    - Multigrain crackers
    - Sesame crackers
    - Rosemary crackers
    - Cheese crackers
- Fresh fruit such as:
    - Grapes
    - Sliced apples
    - Sliced pears
    - Berries (strawberries, raspberries, blackberries)

- Dried fruit such as:
    - Apricots
    - Figs
    - Dates
    - Cranberries
- Nuts such as:
    - Almonds
    - Walnuts
    - Pecans
    - Cashews
- Olives:
    - Kalamata olives
    - Green olives
    - Stuffed olives
- Honey or honeycomb (optional, for drizzling)
- Fig or fruit jam (optional)
- Mustard (optional)
- Pickles or gherkins (optional)
- Fresh herbs for garnish (optional)

Instructions:

1. Arrange the assorted cheeses on a large serving platter or cheese board. Be sure to vary the flavors, textures, and types of cheese for a diverse tasting experience.
2. Place the assorted crackers in small piles or clusters around the cheese on the platter.
3. Arrange the fresh and dried fruits, nuts, and olives in small bowls or clusters around the cheese and crackers on the platter.
4. If using honey or honeycomb, fig or fruit jam, mustard, or pickles, place them in small bowls or ramekins on the platter for dipping or spreading.
5. Optionally, garnish the platter with fresh herbs such as rosemary sprigs or basil leaves for added color and flavor.
6. Serve the assorted cheese and crackers platter as an appetizer at your wedding reception.

This platter offers a beautiful presentation of flavors and textures, and it's sure to be a crowd-pleaser for guests to enjoy throughout the celebration. Enjoy!

Smoked Salmon Crostini with Dill Cream Cheese

Ingredients:

For the dill cream cheese:

- 8 oz cream cheese, softened
- 2 tablespoons fresh dill, finely chopped
- 1 tablespoon lemon juice
- Salt and pepper to taste

For the crostini:

- Baguette or French bread, sliced into 1/2-inch thick rounds
- Olive oil
- Salt and pepper to taste

For assembling:

- Smoked salmon slices
- Fresh dill sprigs, for garnish

Instructions:

1. Preheat your oven to 375°F (190°C). Line a baking sheet with parchment paper.
2. Prepare the dill cream cheese:
    - In a mixing bowl, combine the softened cream cheese, finely chopped fresh dill, lemon juice, salt, and pepper.
    - Mix until well combined and smooth. Taste and adjust seasoning if needed. Set aside.
3. Prepare the crostini:
    - Arrange the baguette or French bread slices on the prepared baking sheet.
    - Brush each slice with olive oil and season with salt and pepper to taste.

- Bake in the preheated oven for 10-12 minutes, or until the bread is lightly toasted and crisp. Remove from the oven and let cool slightly.
4. Assemble the crostini:
    - Spread a generous amount of dill cream cheese onto each toasted bread slice.
5. Top each crostini with a slice of smoked salmon, folding or arranging it attractively on top of the cream cheese.
6. Garnish each crostini with a small sprig of fresh dill.
7. Arrange the smoked salmon crostini on a serving platter and serve immediately.

These smoked salmon crostini with dill cream cheese are sure to impress your wedding guests with their elegant presentation and delicious flavor. Enjoy!

Grilled Vegetable Platter with Herb Dip

Ingredients:

For the grilled vegetables:

- Assorted vegetables such as:
    - Zucchini, sliced lengthwise
    - Bell peppers, sliced into strips
    - Eggplant, sliced into rounds
    - Cherry tomatoes
    - Red onion, sliced into rounds
    - Asparagus spears
    - Mushrooms, whole or halved
- Olive oil
- Salt and pepper to taste
- Fresh herbs such as thyme or rosemary, chopped (optional, for garnish)

For the herb dip:

- 1 cup Greek yogurt or sour cream
- 2 tablespoons mayonnaise
- 1 tablespoon lemon juice
- 2 tablespoons chopped fresh herbs such as dill, parsley, chives, or basil
- 1 clove garlic, minced
- Salt and pepper to taste

Instructions:

1. Preheat your grill to medium-high heat.
2. Prepare the vegetables:
    - In a large bowl, toss the sliced vegetables with olive oil, salt, and pepper until they are evenly coated.
    - If using wooden skewers for the vegetables, soak them in water for about 30 minutes to prevent burning.
3. Grill the vegetables:

- Place the prepared vegetables on the preheated grill. Cook for 3-5 minutes per side, or until they are tender and have grill marks.
- Remove the grilled vegetables from the grill and transfer them to a serving platter.

4. Prepare the herb dip:
   - In a small bowl, mix together the Greek yogurt or sour cream, mayonnaise, lemon juice, chopped fresh herbs, minced garlic, salt, and pepper until well combined.
5. Transfer the herb dip to a serving bowl and place it in the center of the grilled vegetable platter.
6. Optionally, garnish the herb dip with additional chopped fresh herbs.
7. Serve the grilled vegetable platter with herb dip as an appetizer at your wedding reception.

This platter offers a beautiful array of colors and flavors, and the herb dip adds a delicious and creamy accompaniment. Your guests are sure to enjoy this fresh and healthy appetizer option.

Chicken Quesadillas with Salsa and Guacamole

Ingredients:

For the chicken filling:

- 2 boneless, skinless chicken breasts
- 1 tablespoon olive oil
- 1 teaspoon chili powder
- 1 teaspoon cumin
- 1/2 teaspoon garlic powder
- Salt and pepper to taste
- 1 cup shredded cheese (cheddar, Monterey Jack, or a Mexican blend)

For assembling:

- 8 large flour tortillas
- 1 cup salsa (store-bought or homemade)
- 1 cup guacamole (store-bought or homemade)
- Sour cream (optional, for serving)
- Chopped fresh cilantro (optional, for garnish)

Instructions:

1. Preheat the oven to 400°F (200°C). Line a baking sheet with parchment paper.
2. Prepare the chicken filling:
   - Season the chicken breasts with chili powder, cumin, garlic powder, salt, and pepper.
   - Heat olive oil in a skillet over medium-high heat. Cook the chicken breasts for about 6-8 minutes on each side, or until cooked through and no longer pink in the center.
   - Remove the chicken from the skillet and let it rest for a few minutes before shredding it using two forks or slicing it thinly.
3. Assemble the quesadillas:
   - Lay out four tortillas on a flat surface. Sprinkle shredded cheese evenly over each tortilla.

- Divide the cooked chicken evenly among the tortillas, spreading it over one half of each tortilla.
- Fold the tortillas in half over the filling to form half-moon shapes.
4. Cook the quesadillas:
    - Place the assembled quesadillas on the prepared baking sheet.
    - Bake in the preheated oven for 8-10 minutes, or until the tortillas are golden brown and the cheese is melted and bubbly.
5. Serve:
    - Once cooked, remove the quesadillas from the oven and let them cool for a minute.
    - Cut each quesadilla into wedges using a pizza cutter or a sharp knife.
    - Serve the quesadilla wedges with salsa, guacamole, sour cream, and chopped cilantro on the side for dipping or topping.

Enjoy these delicious chicken quesadillas with salsa and guacamole as a flavorful appetizer option at your wedding reception!

Antipasto Skewers with Salami, Olives, and Mozzarella

Ingredients:

- Cherry tomatoes
- Mozzarella balls (bocconcini or ciliegine)
- Salami slices, cut into small pieces
- Black or green olives, pitted
- Basil leaves
- Balsamic glaze (optional, for drizzling)
- Wooden skewers

Instructions:

1. Prepare the ingredients:
    - If the cherry tomatoes are large, cut them in half.
    - Thread the cherry tomatoes, mozzarella balls, salami pieces, olives, and basil leaves onto the wooden skewers in alternating order. You can fold or roll the salami slices before threading them onto the skewers for a decorative touch.
2. Arrange the skewers on a serving platter or tray.
3. Optionally, drizzle balsamic glaze over the skewers for added flavor and presentation.
4. Serve the antipasto skewers with salami, olives, and mozzarella as an appetizer at your wedding reception.

These skewers offer a beautiful presentation of classic Italian flavors, and they're sure to be a hit with your guests. Enjoy!

Mini Quiches with Various Fillings (e.g., spinach, bacon, cheese)

Ingredients:

For the quiche base:

- 1 package (14 oz) refrigerated pie crust dough (or homemade pie crust)
- Cooking spray

For the fillings:

- Spinach filling:
    - 1 cup fresh spinach, chopped
    - 1/4 cup onion, finely chopped
    - 1 clove garlic, minced
    - Salt and pepper to taste
- Bacon and cheese filling:
    - 4 slices bacon, cooked and crumbled
    - 1/2 cup shredded cheddar cheese
- Other options: diced ham, diced cooked chicken, sautéed mushrooms, diced bell peppers, etc.

For the custard:

- 4 large eggs
- 1 cup milk or half-and-half
- Salt and pepper to taste
- Pinch of nutmeg (optional)

Instructions:

1. Preheat your oven to 375°F (190°C). Lightly grease a mini muffin tin with cooking spray.

2. Roll out the pie crust dough on a lightly floured surface. Use a round cookie cutter or a glass to cut out circles slightly larger than the mini muffin tin cups.
3. Press the dough circles into the mini muffin tin cups, shaping them to fit. Prick the bottoms of the dough with a fork to prevent air bubbles.
4. Prepare the fillings:
    - For the spinach filling: In a skillet, sauté the chopped onion and garlic until softened. Add the chopped spinach and cook until wilted. Season with salt and pepper. Remove from heat and let cool.
    - For the bacon and cheese filling: Cook the bacon until crispy, then crumble it. Mix the crumbled bacon with shredded cheddar cheese.
5. Divide the fillings among the mini quiche crusts, filling each about halfway.
6. In a mixing bowl, whisk together the eggs, milk or half-and-half, salt, pepper, and nutmeg (if using) until well combined.
7. Pour the egg mixture over the fillings in each mini quiche crust, filling almost to the top.
8. Bake the mini quiches in the preheated oven for 15-20 minutes, or until the custard is set and the edges of the crust are golden brown.
9. Remove the mini quiches from the oven and let them cool in the muffin tin for a few minutes before carefully removing them to a wire rack to cool completely.
10. Serve the mini quiches with various fillings as an appetizer at your wedding reception.

These mini quiches are not only delicious but also customizable to suit different tastes.

Your guests are sure to love the variety of flavors!

Coconut Shrimp with Mango Dipping Sauce

Ingredients:

For the coconut shrimp:

- 1 lb large shrimp, peeled and deveined, tails left on
- 1 cup sweetened shredded coconut
- 1 cup panko breadcrumbs
- 2 eggs
- 1/2 cup all-purpose flour
- Salt and pepper to taste
- Cooking oil for frying

For the mango dipping sauce:

- 1 ripe mango, peeled and diced
- 1/4 cup mayonnaise
- 1 tablespoon honey
- 1 tablespoon lime juice
- 1 teaspoon Sriracha sauce (optional, for a spicy kick)
- Salt to taste

Instructions:

1. Preheat your oven to 400°F (200°C). Line a baking sheet with parchment paper.
2. Prepare the coconut shrimp:
    - In three separate shallow bowls, place the flour in one, beaten eggs in another, and a mixture of shredded coconut and panko breadcrumbs in the third.
    - Season the shrimp with salt and pepper.
    - Dredge each shrimp in the flour, shaking off any excess. Then dip it into the beaten eggs, and finally coat it with the coconut-panko mixture, pressing gently to adhere.
    - Place the coated shrimp on the prepared baking sheet.
3. Bake the coconut shrimp:

- Drizzle or spray the coated shrimp with cooking oil.
- Bake in the preheated oven for 12-15 minutes, or until the shrimp are cooked through and the coconut coating is golden brown and crispy.
4. Prepare the mango dipping sauce:
    - In a blender or food processor, combine the diced mango, mayonnaise, honey, lime juice, and Sriracha sauce (if using).
    - Blend until smooth. If the sauce is too thick, you can add a little water to reach your desired consistency.
    - Season the sauce with salt to taste.
5. Serve the baked coconut shrimp with the mango dipping sauce on the side.

This combination of crispy coconut shrimp and sweet, tangy mango dipping sauce is sure to be a hit with your wedding guests. Enjoy!

Brie and Raspberry Phyllo Cups

Ingredients:

- 1 package (15 count) mini phyllo pastry shells
- 4 oz Brie cheese, rind removed, cut into small cubes
- 1/4 cup raspberry preserves or jam
- Fresh raspberries, for garnish (optional)
- Fresh mint leaves, for garnish (optional)

Instructions:

1. Preheat your oven to 350°F (175°C). Place the mini phyllo pastry shells on a baking sheet lined with parchment paper.
2. Place a small cube of Brie cheese in the bottom of each phyllo pastry shell.
3. Spoon a small amount of raspberry preserves or jam on top of the Brie cheese in each pastry shell.
4. Bake the filled phyllo pastry shells in the preheated oven for 5-7 minutes, or until the cheese is melted and the pastry shells are golden brown and crispy.
5. Remove the baked phyllo cups from the oven and let them cool slightly.
6. Garnish each phyllo cup with a fresh raspberry and a small mint leaf, if desired.
7. Serve the Brie and raspberry phyllo cups immediately as an appetizer at your wedding reception.

These elegant and flavorful appetizers are sure to impress your guests with their combination of creamy Brie cheese and sweet raspberry flavor. Enjoy!

Cucumber Cups with Herbed Cream Cheese

Ingredients:

- 2 large English cucumbers
- 8 oz cream cheese, softened
- 2 tablespoons chopped fresh herbs (such as dill, chives, parsley, or a combination)
- 1 tablespoon lemon juice
- Salt and pepper to taste
- Optional garnish: additional fresh herbs, lemon zest, or paprika

Instructions:

1. Wash the cucumbers thoroughly and pat them dry with paper towels. Trim off the ends of each cucumber.
2. Cut the cucumbers into 1-inch thick slices. Use a small melon baller or a teaspoon to carefully scoop out the seeds from the center of each cucumber slice, creating a small well or cup. Be careful not to scoop all the way through the bottom of the cucumber slice.
3. In a mixing bowl, combine the softened cream cheese, chopped fresh herbs, lemon juice, salt, and pepper. Stir until the herbs are evenly distributed throughout the cream cheese mixture.
4. Spoon or pipe the herbed cream cheese mixture into each cucumber cup, filling them to the top.
5. Optionally, garnish each cucumber cup with additional fresh herbs, lemon zest, or a sprinkle of paprika for added color and flavor.
6. Arrange the filled cucumber cups on a serving platter and refrigerate until ready to serve.
7. Serve the cucumber cups with herbed cream cheese as an appetizer at your wedding reception.

These cucumber cups are not only delicious but also beautifully presented, making them a perfect addition to any wedding menu. Enjoy!

Teriyaki Glazed Salmon Skewers

Ingredients:

- 1 lb salmon fillet, skin removed, cut into 1-inch cubes
- 1/4 cup soy sauce
- 2 tablespoons brown sugar
- 2 tablespoons honey
- 2 cloves garlic, minced
- 1 teaspoon grated ginger
- 1 tablespoon rice vinegar
- 1 tablespoon sesame oil
- Wooden skewers, soaked in water for 30 minutes

Optional garnishes:

- Thinly sliced green onions
- Sesame seeds
- Sliced red chili peppers
- Chopped cilantro

Instructions:

1. In a small saucepan, combine the soy sauce, brown sugar, honey, minced garlic, grated ginger, rice vinegar, and sesame oil. Cook over medium heat, stirring occasionally, until the sugar has dissolved and the sauce has thickened slightly, about 5-7 minutes. Remove from heat and let cool.
2. Place the salmon cubes in a shallow dish or resealable plastic bag. Pour half of the teriyaki sauce over the salmon, reserving the other half for basting and serving. Toss the salmon gently to coat in the sauce. Marinate in the refrigerator for at least 30 minutes, or up to 2 hours.
3. Preheat your grill or grill pan to medium-high heat.
4. Thread the marinated salmon cubes onto the soaked wooden skewers, leaving a little space between each piece.

5. Brush the grill grates lightly with oil to prevent sticking. Place the salmon skewers on the preheated grill and cook for 3-4 minutes per side, or until the salmon is cooked through and has grill marks.
6. While grilling, baste the salmon skewers with the reserved teriyaki sauce using a brush.
7. Once cooked, remove the salmon skewers from the grill and transfer them to a serving platter.
8. Garnish the teriyaki glazed salmon skewers with thinly sliced green onions, sesame seeds, sliced red chili peppers, and chopped cilantro, if desired.
9. Serve the salmon skewers immediately with the remaining teriyaki sauce on the side for dipping.

These teriyaki glazed salmon skewers are sure to be a hit with your wedding guests, with their delicious flavor and beautiful presentation. Enjoy!

Assorted Sushi Rolls

Ingredients:

For the sushi rice:

- 2 cups sushi rice
- 2 1/2 cups water
- 1/2 cup rice vinegar
- 2 tablespoons sugar
- 1 teaspoon salt

For the assorted fillings:

- Nori (seaweed) sheets
- Assorted fillings such as:
    - Sliced raw fish (salmon, tuna, yellowtail)
    - Cooked shrimp
    - Crab meat
    - Avocado
    - Cucumber
    - Carrot, thinly sliced
    - Cream cheese
    - Scallions
    - Sesame seeds
    - Tempura shrimp
    - Spicy mayo
    - Eel sauce
    - Pickled ginger
    - Wasabi
    - Soy sauce

Instructions:

1. Prepare the sushi rice:

- Rinse the sushi rice under cold water until the water runs clear. Drain well.
- In a rice cooker or a pot, combine the rinsed rice and water. Cook according to the rice cooker instructions or bring to a boil, then reduce the heat to low, cover, and simmer for 18-20 minutes until the rice is cooked and tender.
- In a small saucepan, combine the rice vinegar, sugar, and salt. Heat over low heat until the sugar and salt dissolve.
- Transfer the cooked rice to a large bowl and gently fold in the seasoned vinegar mixture until well combined. Let the rice cool to room temperature.

2. Prepare the fillings:
   - Slice the raw fish thinly against the grain.
   - Cook and shell the shrimp, if using.
   - Cut the avocado into thin slices.
   - Julienne the cucumber and carrot into thin strips.
   - Prepare any other desired fillings.

3. Assemble the sushi rolls:
   - Place a sheet of nori on a bamboo sushi rolling mat, shiny side down.
   - Wet your hands with water to prevent sticking, then spread a thin layer of sushi rice evenly over the nori, leaving about a 1-inch border at the top edge.
   - Arrange your desired fillings in a line across the bottom third of the rice-covered nori sheet.
   - Using the bamboo mat, roll the sushi tightly away from you, pressing gently to seal. Wet the top border of the nori with a little water to help seal the roll.
   - Use a sharp knife to slice the sushi roll into 6-8 pieces, wiping the knife clean between cuts.

4. Repeat the process with the remaining nori sheets and fillings to make a variety of sushi rolls.

5. Serve the assorted sushi rolls with pickled ginger, wasabi, and soy sauce on the side.

Enjoy your assortment of delicious sushi rolls at your wedding reception!

Meat and Cheese Charcuterie Board

Ingredients:

For the charcuterie board:

- Assorted cured meats such as:
    - Prosciutto
    - Salami
    - Chorizo
    - Pepperoni
    - Soppressata
- Assorted cheeses such as:
    - Brie
    - Camembert
    - Manchego
    - Cheddar
    - Gouda
    - Blue cheese
- Assorted crackers and breadsticks
- Fresh fruits such as grapes, figs, and berries
- Dried fruits such as apricots, dates, and figs
- Nuts such as almonds, walnuts, and cashews
- Olives and pickles
- Honey or fig jam for drizzling or spreading
- Mustard or chutney for dipping

Instructions:

1. Arrange the cured meats on the charcuterie board, folding or rolling them for an attractive presentation. Leave some space between each type of meat for easy grabbing.
2. Place the assorted cheeses on the board, slicing or cubing some and leaving others whole for variety. Spread them out evenly around the meats.
3. Fill in the gaps on the board with crackers, breadsticks, and fresh and dried fruits. This adds color and texture to the spread.

4. Add small bowls or ramekins of olives, pickles, nuts, and dips such as honey, fig jam, mustard, or chutney. Place them strategically around the board for easy access.
5. Garnish the board with fresh herbs, such as rosemary or thyme sprigs, for a decorative touch.
6. Consider labeling the different meats and cheeses on the board, especially if there are unique or unfamiliar varieties.
7. Serve the meat and cheese charcuterie board as a stunning appetizer at your wedding reception, allowing guests to help themselves to their favorite combinations.

This meat and cheese charcuterie board is sure to impress your guests with its variety of flavors and elegant presentation. Enjoy!

Crab Stuffed Mushrooms

Ingredients:

- 24 large mushrooms, cleaned and stems removed
- 8 oz lump crab meat, drained and picked over for shells
- 1/2 cup cream cheese, softened
- 1/4 cup grated Parmesan cheese
- 2 cloves garlic, minced
- 2 tablespoons chopped fresh parsley
- 1 tablespoon lemon juice
- Salt and pepper to taste
- Olive oil, for drizzling
- Optional: additional Parmesan cheese for topping

Instructions:

1. Preheat your oven to 375°F (190°C). Line a baking sheet with parchment paper.
2. In a mixing bowl, combine the lump crab meat, softened cream cheese, grated Parmesan cheese, minced garlic, chopped parsley, lemon juice, salt, and pepper. Mix until well combined.
3. Fill each mushroom cap with a spoonful of the crab mixture, pressing gently to pack it in.
4. Place the stuffed mushrooms on the prepared baking sheet. Drizzle a little olive oil over the top of each mushroom.
5. Optionally, sprinkle additional Parmesan cheese over the stuffed mushrooms for extra flavor.
6. Bake the crab stuffed mushrooms in the preheated oven for 15-20 minutes, or until the mushrooms are tender and the filling is heated through and lightly golden on top.
7. Remove the stuffed mushrooms from the oven and let them cool slightly before serving.
8. Serve the crab stuffed mushrooms warm as an appetizer at your wedding reception.

These crab stuffed mushrooms are sure to be a hit with your guests, with their savory filling and elegant presentation. Enjoy!

Spanakopita Triangles (Spinach and Feta in Filo Pastry)

Ingredients:

- 1 package (about 16 oz) frozen chopped spinach, thawed and drained
- 1 cup crumbled feta cheese
- 1/4 cup grated Parmesan cheese
- 1/4 cup chopped fresh dill
- 1/4 cup chopped fresh parsley
- 2 green onions, finely chopped
- 2 cloves garlic, minced
- Salt and pepper to taste
- 1/4 cup olive oil, plus more for brushing
- 1 package (about 16 oz) filo pastry sheets, thawed according to package instructions
- Melted butter or olive oil for brushing

Instructions:

1. Preheat your oven to 375°F (190°C). Line a baking sheet with parchment paper.
2. In a large mixing bowl, combine the thawed and drained chopped spinach, crumbled feta cheese, grated Parmesan cheese, chopped dill, chopped parsley, chopped green onions, minced garlic, salt, and pepper. Mix well to combine.
3. Place one sheet of filo pastry on a clean work surface and brush it lightly with olive oil or melted butter. Place another sheet of filo pastry on top and brush with oil or butter. Repeat with a third sheet of filo pastry.
4. Cut the layered filo pastry into 3-inch wide strips lengthwise.
5. Place a spoonful of the spinach and feta mixture at the bottom of each strip of filo pastry.
6. Fold one corner of the filo pastry over the filling to form a triangle. Continue folding the pastry over itself, as you would fold a flag, until you reach the end of the strip. Brush the outside of the triangle with olive oil or melted butter to seal.
7. Repeat the process with the remaining filo pastry strips and spinach-feta filling.
8. Place the assembled spanakopita triangles on the prepared baking sheet.
9. Bake in the preheated oven for 20-25 minutes, or until the triangles are golden brown and crispy.
10. Remove from the oven and let cool slightly before serving.

11. Serve the spanakopita triangles warm as an appetizer at your wedding reception.

Enjoy these delicious spinach and feta-filled filo pastry triangles with your guests!

Chicken and Waffle Sliders with Maple Syrup

Ingredients:

For the chicken:

- 1 lb boneless, skinless chicken breasts
- 1 cup buttermilk
- 1 teaspoon salt
- 1/2 teaspoon black pepper
- 1/2 teaspoon paprika
- 1/4 teaspoon garlic powder
- 1/4 teaspoon onion powder
- 1 cup all-purpose flour
- Vegetable oil, for frying

For the waffles:

- 2 cups all-purpose flour
- 2 tablespoons granulated sugar
- 1 tablespoon baking powder
- 1/2 teaspoon salt
- 2 large eggs
- 1 3/4 cups milk
- 1/2 cup unsalted butter, melted
- Vegetable oil or non-stick cooking spray, for greasing the waffle iron

For serving:

- Maple syrup
- Optional: sliced strawberries or powdered sugar for garnish

Instructions:

1. Prepare the chicken:
   - Cut the chicken breasts into small, slider-sized pieces.
   - In a bowl, whisk together the buttermilk, salt, pepper, paprika, garlic powder, and onion powder. Add the chicken pieces to the buttermilk mixture, making sure they are well coated. Cover and refrigerate for at least 30 minutes, or up to 4 hours.
2. Prepare the waffles:
   - Preheat your waffle iron according to the manufacturer's instructions.
   - In a large bowl, whisk together the flour, sugar, baking powder, and salt.
   - In another bowl, whisk together the eggs, milk, and melted butter.
   - Pour the wet ingredients into the dry ingredients and stir until just combined. Do not overmix; a few lumps are okay.
   - Grease the waffle iron with oil or non-stick cooking spray. Pour the batter onto the preheated waffle iron and cook according to the manufacturer's instructions, until the waffles are golden brown and crisp. Repeat with the remaining batter.
3. Fry the chicken:
   - In a shallow dish, place the flour. Dredge each marinated chicken piece in the flour, shaking off any excess.
   - In a large skillet, heat vegetable oil over medium-high heat. Once hot, add the chicken pieces in batches and fry until golden brown and cooked through, about 3-4 minutes per side. Transfer the cooked chicken to a paper towel-lined plate to drain excess oil.
4. Assemble the sliders:
   - Cut each waffle into slider-sized squares.
   - Place a piece of fried chicken on the bottom half of each waffle square.
   - Drizzle maple syrup over the chicken, then top with the remaining waffle squares.
   - Secure each slider with a toothpick if desired.
   - Optionally, garnish with sliced strawberries or a dusting of powdered sugar.
5. Serve the chicken and waffle sliders warm, with extra maple syrup on the side for dipping.

Enjoy these delightful chicken and waffle sliders with maple syrup at your wedding reception!

Tuna Tartare on Wonton Crisps

Ingredients:

For the tuna tartare:

- 8 oz sushi-grade tuna, finely diced
- 2 tablespoons soy sauce
- 1 tablespoon sesame oil
- 1 tablespoon rice vinegar
- 1 teaspoon honey or agave nectar
- 1 teaspoon grated fresh ginger
- 1 teaspoon finely chopped chives or green onions
- 1 teaspoon sesame seeds (optional)
- Salt and pepper to taste

For the wonton crisps:

- 12 wonton wrappers
- Vegetable oil for frying

For garnish:

- Thinly sliced green onions
- Sesame seeds
- Avocado slices
- Sriracha mayo or wasabi mayo (optional)

Instructions:

1. Prepare the tuna tartare:
    - In a mixing bowl, combine the diced tuna, soy sauce, sesame oil, rice vinegar, honey or agave nectar, grated ginger, chopped chives or green onions, sesame seeds (if using), salt, and pepper. Mix well to combine.

Taste and adjust seasoning if necessary. Cover and refrigerate while you prepare the wonton crisps.
2. Prepare the wonton crisps:
   - Cut each wonton wrapper into quarters to make small triangles.
   - Heat vegetable oil in a deep skillet or pot over medium-high heat until it reaches 350°F (175°C).
   - Carefully add the wonton triangles to the hot oil in batches, making sure not to overcrowd the pan. Fry for about 1-2 minutes on each side, or until golden brown and crispy.
   - Use a slotted spoon to transfer the fried wonton crisps to a paper towel-lined plate to drain excess oil. Allow them to cool completely before assembling.
3. Assemble the tuna tartare on wonton crisps:
   - Spoon a small amount of the chilled tuna tartare onto each wonton crisp.
   - Garnish with thinly sliced green onions, sesame seeds, and avocado slices.
   - Optionally, drizzle with sriracha mayo or wasabi mayo for an extra kick.
4. Serve the tuna tartare on wonton crisps immediately as an elegant appetizer at your wedding reception.

These tuna tartare on wonton crisps are sure to impress your guests with their fresh flavors and crunchy texture. Enjoy!

Bacon-Wrapped Scallops

Ingredients:

- 12 large sea scallops, cleaned and patted dry
- 6 slices of bacon, cut in half crosswise
- Salt and pepper to taste
- Toothpicks

Instructions:

1. Preheat your oven to 400°F (200°C). Line a baking sheet with aluminum foil and place a wire rack on top.
2. Season each scallop with salt and pepper.
3. Wrap each scallop with a half slice of bacon, securing it with a toothpick. Make sure the bacon completely covers the scallop.
4. Place the bacon-wrapped scallops on the prepared baking sheet, spacing them evenly apart.
5. Bake in the preheated oven for 15-20 minutes, or until the bacon is crispy and the scallops are cooked through. You can also broil them for the last 1-2 minutes to crisp up the bacon further.
6. Once cooked, remove the toothpicks from the bacon-wrapped scallops.
7. Serve the bacon-wrapped scallops hot as an appetizer at your wedding reception.

These bacon-wrapped scallops are sure to be a hit with your guests, with their irresistible combination of smoky bacon and tender scallops. Enjoy!

Assorted Bruschetta Trio (Tomato Basil, Olive Tapenade, Fig and Prosciutto)

1. Tomato Basil Bruschetta:

Ingredients:

- 2 large ripe tomatoes, diced

- 2 cloves garlic, minced
- 1/4 cup fresh basil leaves, chopped
- 2 tablespoons extra virgin olive oil
- Salt and pepper to taste
- Baguette, sliced and toasted

Instructions:

a. In a bowl, combine the diced tomatoes, minced garlic, chopped basil, and extra virgin olive oil.

b. Season with salt and pepper to taste and mix well.

c. Spoon the tomato basil mixture onto toasted baguette slices.

d. Optionally, drizzle with a little more olive oil before serving.

2. Olive Tapenade Bruschetta:

Ingredients:

- 1 cup pitted black olives
- 2 tablespoons capers
- 1 clove garlic, minced
- 1 tablespoon lemon juice
- 2 tablespoons extra virgin olive oil
- Baguette, sliced and toasted

Instructions:

a. In a food processor, combine the pitted black olives, capers, minced garlic, lemon juice, and extra virgin olive oil.

b. Pulse until the mixture is finely chopped and reaches your desired consistency.

c. Spoon the olive tapenade onto toasted baguette slices.

d. Optionally, garnish with a few additional capers or a drizzle of olive oil before serving.

3. Fig and Prosciutto Bruschetta:

Ingredients:

- 6-8 fresh figs, sliced
- 4 ounces prosciutto, thinly sliced
- 4 ounces goat cheese
- Honey for drizzling
- Baguette, sliced and toasted

Instructions:

a. Spread a thin layer of goat cheese onto each toasted baguette slice.

b. Top with a slice of prosciutto and a few slices of fresh fig.

c. Drizzle with honey for a touch of sweetness.

d. Optionally, garnish with a small basil leaf or a sprinkle of black pepper before serving.

Arrange the assorted bruschetta trio on a platter, and serve them as an elegant appetizer at your wedding reception. Your guests will love the variety of flavors and textures!

Mini Lobster Rolls

Ingredients:

- 1 lb cooked lobster meat, chopped into small pieces
- 1/4 cup mayonnaise
- 1 tablespoon lemon juice
- 1 tablespoon chopped fresh chives
- Salt and pepper to taste
- Mini brioche rolls or dinner rolls, split and lightly toasted
- Butter, for toasting the rolls
- Lettuce leaves, torn into small pieces (optional)
- Lemon wedges, for garnish

Instructions:

1. In a mixing bowl, combine the chopped lobster meat, mayonnaise, lemon juice, chopped chives, salt, and pepper. Mix well until the lobster meat is evenly coated with the mayonnaise mixture. Adjust seasoning to taste.
2. Heat a skillet over medium heat and melt a little butter. Place the split mini rolls, cut side down, in the skillet and toast until lightly golden brown. Remove from the skillet and set aside.
3. If using lettuce leaves, place a small piece on the bottom half of each toasted roll.
4. Spoon the lobster mixture onto the lettuce or directly onto the bottom half of each roll.
5. Place the top half of each roll over the lobster mixture to create mini lobster rolls.
6. Optionally, insert a small skewer or toothpick through the center of each mini lobster roll to hold them together.
7. Garnish the mini lobster rolls with lemon wedges on the side.
8. Serve the mini lobster rolls immediately as an elegant appetizer at your wedding reception.

These mini lobster rolls are sure to impress your guests with their delicious flavor and elegant presentation. Enjoy!

Gourmet Macaroni and Cheese Bites

Ingredients:

- 8 oz elbow macaroni
- 2 tablespoons unsalted butter
- 2 tablespoons all-purpose flour
- 1 cup whole milk
- 1 cup shredded sharp cheddar cheese
- 1/2 cup shredded Gruyere cheese
- 1/4 cup grated Parmesan cheese
- 1/4 teaspoon paprika
- Salt and pepper to taste
- 2 large eggs
- 1/2 cup Panko breadcrumbs
- Cooking spray

Instructions:

1. Preheat your oven to 375°F (190°C). Grease a mini muffin tin with cooking spray and set aside.
2. Cook the elbow macaroni according to the package instructions until al dente. Drain and set aside.
3. In a large saucepan, melt the butter over medium heat. Stir in the flour and cook for 1-2 minutes, stirring constantly, until smooth and bubbly.
4. Gradually whisk in the milk and cook, stirring constantly, until the mixture thickens and comes to a simmer.
5. Reduce the heat to low and stir in the shredded cheddar cheese, shredded Gruyere cheese, grated Parmesan cheese, paprika, salt, and pepper. Stir until the cheese is melted and the sauce is smooth.
6. Remove the saucepan from the heat and stir in the cooked macaroni until well coated.
7. In a small bowl, lightly beat the eggs. Stir the beaten eggs into the macaroni and cheese mixture until evenly distributed.
8. Using a spoon, fill each mini muffin cup with the macaroni and cheese mixture, pressing down gently to compact it.

9. In a separate small bowl, mix the Panko breadcrumbs with a little melted butter or olive oil until evenly coated.
10. Sprinkle the Panko breadcrumbs evenly over the tops of the macaroni and cheese cups.
11. Bake in the preheated oven for 15-20 minutes, or until the tops are golden brown and crispy.
12. Remove from the oven and let cool for a few minutes before carefully removing the macaroni and cheese bites from the muffin tin.
13. Serve the gourmet macaroni and cheese bites warm as an appetizer at your wedding reception.

These gourmet macaroni and cheese bites are sure to be a hit with your guests, with their creamy texture and crispy topping. Enjoy!

Chicken Caesar Salad Bites in Parmesan Cups

Ingredients:

For the Parmesan Cups:

- 1 cup grated Parmesan cheese

For the Chicken Caesar Salad:

- 2 boneless, skinless chicken breasts
- Salt and pepper to taste
- Olive oil
- 1 head of romaine lettuce, chopped
- 1/2 cup Caesar salad dressing (store-bought or homemade)
- 1/4 cup grated Parmesan cheese
- Croutons (optional)
- Cherry tomatoes, halved (optional)

Instructions:

1. Preheat your oven to 375°F (190°C). Line a baking sheet with parchment paper.
2. Make the Parmesan cups:
    - On the prepared baking sheet, evenly distribute the grated Parmesan cheese into 4 circles, leaving space between each circle.
    - Flatten and spread the cheese into thin, even layers, forming circles about 4 inches in diameter.
    - Bake in the preheated oven for 5-7 minutes, or until the edges of the cheese are golden brown and crispy.
    - Remove from the oven and let them cool for a minute or two.
3. Carefully lift the Parmesan circles and drape them over the bottom side of a muffin tin or small glasses, forming cups. Press gently to shape the cups. Let them cool completely to set their shape.
4. Prepare the chicken:
    - Season the chicken breasts with salt and pepper on both sides.

- Heat a skillet over medium-high heat and add a little olive oil. Once hot, add the chicken breasts and cook for about 5-7 minutes per side, or until cooked through and golden brown on the outside.
- Remove from the skillet and let them cool for a few minutes before slicing them into thin strips or bite-sized pieces.

5. Make the Chicken Caesar Salad:
   - In a large mixing bowl, combine the chopped romaine lettuce, Caesar salad dressing, and grated Parmesan cheese. Toss until the lettuce is evenly coated with the dressing.
   - Add the sliced chicken to the bowl and gently toss to combine.
6. Assemble the Chicken Caesar Salad Bites:
   - Spoon the chicken Caesar salad mixture into the Parmesan cups, dividing it evenly among the cups.
   - Garnish with croutons and cherry tomato halves if desired.
7. Serve the Chicken Caesar Salad Bites immediately as an elegant appetizer at your wedding reception.

These Chicken Caesar Salad Bites in Parmesan Cups are not only visually stunning but also bursting with flavor. Enjoy the combination of creamy dressing, tender chicken, and crispy Parmesan cups!

Beef Sliders with Caramelized Onions and Gruyère Cheese

Ingredients:

For the sliders:

- 1 lb ground beef (preferably 80/20 blend)
- Salt and pepper to taste
- Slider buns or dinner rolls, sliced
- Gruyère cheese, sliced

For the caramelized onions:

- 2 large onions, thinly sliced
- 2 tablespoons butter
- 1 tablespoon olive oil
- Salt and pepper to taste
- 1 tablespoon brown sugar (optional)

Instructions:

1. Prepare the caramelized onions:
    - Heat the butter and olive oil in a large skillet over medium heat.
    - Add the sliced onions to the skillet and cook, stirring occasionally, until they begin to soften, about 5-7 minutes.
    - Reduce the heat to medium-low and continue cooking the onions, stirring occasionally, until they are golden brown and caramelized, about 20-30 minutes.
    - If using, sprinkle the brown sugar over the onions during the last 10 minutes of cooking to enhance caramelization.
    - Season the caramelized onions with salt and pepper to taste. Remove from heat and set aside.
2. Prepare the beef sliders:
    - Divide the ground beef into equal-sized portions and form them into small patties slightly larger than the diameter of the slider buns.
    - Season both sides of the beef patties with salt and pepper.

- Heat a grill or skillet over medium-high heat. Cook the beef patties for 2-3 minutes on each side, or until they reach your desired level of doneness.
- During the last minute of cooking, place a slice of Gruyère cheese on top of each beef patty and allow it to melt.
3. Assemble the sliders:
    - Place a beef patty with melted Gruyère cheese on the bottom half of each slider bun.
    - Top each patty with a generous spoonful of caramelized onions.
    - Place the top half of each slider bun on top of the onions to complete the sliders.
4. Secure the sliders with toothpicks if necessary and serve them warm as an appetizer at your wedding reception.

These beef sliders with caramelized onions and Gruyère cheese are sure to be a hit with your guests, with their juicy beef, sweet onions, and melted cheese. Enjoy!

Mushroom Risotto Balls

Ingredients:

For the mushroom risotto:

- 1 cup Arborio rice
- 4 cups chicken or vegetable broth
- 2 tablespoons olive oil
- 1 small onion, finely chopped
- 2 cloves garlic, minced
- 8 oz mushrooms, finely chopped (you can use any variety you like)
- 1/2 cup dry white wine (optional)
- 1/2 cup grated Parmesan cheese
- Salt and pepper to taste
- 2 tablespoons chopped fresh parsley (optional)

For coating and frying:

- 1 cup all-purpose flour
- 2 large eggs, beaten
- 1 cup breadcrumbs
- Vegetable oil for frying

Instructions:

1. Prepare the mushroom risotto:
    - In a saucepan, heat the chicken or vegetable broth over medium heat until simmering. Reduce the heat to low to keep it warm.
    - In a large skillet, heat the olive oil over medium heat. Add the chopped onion and garlic and sauté until softened, about 2-3 minutes.
    - Add the chopped mushrooms to the skillet and cook until they release their moisture and become golden brown, about 5-7 minutes.
    - Add the Arborio rice to the skillet and toast it for 1-2 minutes, stirring constantly.

- If using, pour in the white wine and cook until it is absorbed by the rice, stirring constantly.
- Begin adding the warm broth to the skillet, one ladleful at a time, stirring frequently. Wait until each addition of broth is absorbed before adding the next.
- Continue adding broth and stirring until the rice is creamy and tender, but still slightly firm to the bite (al dente), about 20-25 minutes.
- Remove the skillet from the heat and stir in the grated Parmesan cheese. Season with salt and pepper to taste. If desired, stir in the chopped fresh parsley.
2. Let the risotto cool to room temperature or refrigerate it until firm, at least 1 hour or overnight.
3. Shape the risotto balls:
   - Using your hands, scoop out tablespoon-sized portions of the cooled risotto and roll them into balls. If the risotto is too sticky, wet your hands with water to prevent sticking.
4. Prepare the coating:
   - Place the flour, beaten eggs, and breadcrumbs in three separate shallow bowls.
5. Dip each risotto ball into the flour, shaking off any excess. Then, dip it into the beaten eggs, ensuring it is evenly coated. Finally, roll it in the breadcrumbs, pressing gently to adhere. Place the coated risotto balls on a baking sheet lined with parchment paper.
6. Fry the risotto balls:
   - In a deep skillet or pot, heat vegetable oil to 350°F (175°C). Carefully add a few risotto balls to the hot oil and fry until golden brown and crispy, about 2-3 minutes. Avoid overcrowding the skillet to ensure even frying.
   - Use a slotted spoon to transfer the fried risotto balls to a paper towel-lined plate to drain excess oil. Repeat with the remaining risotto balls.
7. Serve the mushroom risotto balls hot as an appetizer at your wedding reception.

These mushroom risotto balls are crispy on the outside and creamy on the inside, with a rich mushroom flavor that your guests will love. Enjoy!

Stuffed Jalapeño Poppers with Cream Cheese and Bacon

Ingredients:

- 12 large jalapeño peppers
- 8 oz cream cheese, softened
- 1 cup shredded cheddar cheese
- 6 slices of bacon, cooked until crispy and crumbled
- 1 teaspoon garlic powder
- 1/2 teaspoon onion powder
- Salt and pepper to taste
- Toothpicks or cocktail sticks

Instructions:

1. Preheat your oven to 375°F (190°C). Line a baking sheet with parchment paper and set aside.
2. Slice the jalapeño peppers in half lengthwise and remove the seeds and membranes. You can use a spoon or small knife to scrape them out. Be sure to wear gloves or wash your hands thoroughly afterward to avoid irritation from the peppers' oils.
3. In a mixing bowl, combine the softened cream cheese, shredded cheddar cheese, crumbled bacon, garlic powder, onion powder, salt, and pepper. Mix until well combined.
4. Using a spoon or a small spatula, fill each jalapeño half with the cream cheese mixture, pressing it down gently to fill the cavity.
5. Place the stuffed jalapeño halves on the prepared baking sheet.
6. If desired, secure each stuffed jalapeño half with a toothpick or cocktail stick to help keep the filling in place during baking.
7. Bake in the preheated oven for 20-25 minutes, or until the jalapeños are softened and the cheese is melted and bubbly.
8. Remove from the oven and let the stuffed jalapeño poppers cool for a few minutes before serving.
9. Serve the stuffed jalapeño poppers warm as an appetizer at your wedding reception.

These stuffed jalapeño poppers are sure to be a hit with your guests, with their spicy kick, creamy cheese filling, and savory bacon flavor. Enjoy!

Mini Croque Monsieur Bites

Ingredients:

- 12 slices of white bread (preferably sandwich bread), crusts removed
- 6 slices of ham, thinly sliced
- 6 slices of Gruyère cheese (or any Swiss cheese), thinly sliced
- 2 tablespoons unsalted butter
- 2 tablespoons all-purpose flour
- 1 cup whole milk
- 1/2 cup grated Gruyère cheese (or any Swiss cheese)
- 1/4 teaspoon nutmeg
- Salt and pepper to taste
- Dijon mustard for serving (optional)
- Toothpicks or cocktail sticks

Instructions:

1. Preheat your oven to 375°F (190°C). Line a baking sheet with parchment paper and set aside.
2. Prepare the béchamel sauce:
   - In a saucepan, melt the butter over medium heat. Add the flour and cook, stirring constantly, for 1-2 minutes to form a roux.
   - Gradually whisk in the milk, ensuring no lumps form.
   - Cook the mixture, stirring constantly, until it thickens and comes to a simmer.
   - Remove the saucepan from the heat and stir in the grated Gruyère cheese until melted and smooth.
   - Season the sauce with nutmeg, salt, and pepper to taste. Set aside.
3. Assemble the mini Croque Monsieur bites:
   - Place the slices of bread on a flat surface. Spread a thin layer of Dijon mustard on half of the bread slices (if using).
   - Top each mustard-coated slice of bread with a slice of ham and a slice of Gruyère cheese. Place the remaining bread slices on top to form sandwiches.
   - Using a sharp knife, cut each sandwich into quarters to make mini triangles.

4. Dip each mini Croque Monsieur triangle into the prepared béchamel sauce, ensuring they are evenly coated on all sides.
5. Place the coated mini Croque Monsieur triangles on the prepared baking sheet.
6. Bake in the preheated oven for 15-20 minutes, or until the tops are golden brown and crispy.
7. Remove from the oven and let the mini Croque Monsieur bites cool for a few minutes before serving.
8. Insert toothpicks or cocktail sticks into each mini Croque Monsieur bite for easy serving.
9. Serve the mini Croque Monsieur bites warm as an appetizer at your wedding reception.

These mini Croque Monsieur bites are sure to impress your guests with their delicious flavor and elegant presentation. Enjoy!

Falafel Balls with Tzatziki Sauce

Ingredients:

For the falafel balls:

- 2 cups cooked chickpeas (canned or cooked from dry)
- 1 small onion, roughly chopped
- 3 cloves garlic, minced
- 1/4 cup fresh parsley, chopped
- 1/4 cup fresh cilantro, chopped
- 1 teaspoon ground cumin
- 1 teaspoon ground coriander
- 1/2 teaspoon paprika
- 1/4 teaspoon cayenne pepper (optional, for extra heat)
- Salt and pepper to taste
- 2 tablespoons all-purpose flour (or chickpea flour for a gluten-free option)
- 1 teaspoon baking powder
- Vegetable oil for frying

For the tzatziki sauce:

- 1 cup Greek yogurt
- 1/2 cucumber, grated and squeezed to remove excess moisture
- 1 clove garlic, minced
- 1 tablespoon lemon juice
- 1 tablespoon chopped fresh dill (or 1 teaspoon dried dill)
- Salt and pepper to taste

Instructions:

1. Prepare the falafel mixture:
    - In a food processor, combine the cooked chickpeas, onion, garlic, parsley, cilantro, cumin, coriander, paprika, cayenne pepper (if using), salt, and pepper.

- Pulse the mixture until it is well combined but still slightly chunky. You may need to scrape down the sides of the food processor bowl occasionally.
- Transfer the falafel mixture to a mixing bowl.

2. Add the flour and baking powder to the falafel mixture and mix until everything is well combined. The mixture should be thick and hold together easily. If it's too dry, you can add a little water; if it's too wet, you can add more flour.
3. Shape the falafel mixture into small balls, about 1 inch in diameter, and place them on a baking sheet lined with parchment paper.
4. Heat vegetable oil in a deep skillet or pot over medium-high heat until it reaches 350°F (175°C).
5. Carefully add the falafel balls to the hot oil in batches, making sure not to overcrowd the pan. Fry the falafel balls for 2-3 minutes, or until they are golden brown and crispy on the outside. Use a slotted spoon to transfer them to a plate lined with paper towels to drain excess oil.
6. While the falafel balls are frying, prepare the tzatziki sauce:
    - In a bowl, combine the Greek yogurt, grated cucumber, minced garlic, lemon juice, chopped dill, salt, and pepper. Stir until well combined. Taste and adjust seasoning as needed.
7. Serve the falafel balls warm with the tzatziki sauce on the side for dipping.
8. Garnish with additional chopped fresh herbs or a squeeze of lemon juice if desired.

These falafel balls with tzatziki sauce are best served fresh and are sure to be a hit with your wedding guests! Enjoy!

Peking Duck Pancakes with Hoisin Sauce

Ingredients:

For the Peking duck:

- 1 whole Peking duck (about 5-6 lbs)
- 1/4 cup hoisin sauce
- 2 tablespoons soy sauce
- 1 tablespoon honey
- 2 cloves garlic, minced
- 1 teaspoon Chinese five-spice powder
- Salt and pepper to taste
- 12-16 Chinese pancakes (available at Asian grocery stores) or flour tortillas

For the hoisin sauce:

- 1/2 cup hoisin sauce
- 2 tablespoons soy sauce
- 1 tablespoon rice vinegar
- 1 tablespoon honey
- 1 teaspoon sesame oil

For serving:

- Thinly sliced green onions (optional)
- Thinly sliced cucumbers (optional)

Instructions:

1. Preheat your oven to 375°F (190°C). Place a wire rack on a baking sheet lined with aluminum foil or parchment paper.
2. In a small bowl, mix together the hoisin sauce, soy sauce, honey, minced garlic, Chinese five-spice powder, salt, and pepper to create the marinade for the duck.

3. Rinse the duck inside and out with cold water and pat dry with paper towels. Use a sharp knife to prick the skin of the duck all over, being careful not to pierce the meat.
4. Brush the duck all over, inside and out, with the hoisin sauce marinade. Make sure to coat it evenly.
5. Place the duck on the wire rack on the prepared baking sheet, breast side up.
6. Roast the duck in the preheated oven for about 1 1/2 to 2 hours, or until the skin is crispy and golden brown and the internal temperature reaches 165°F (74°C). If the skin starts to brown too quickly, cover it loosely with aluminum foil.
7. While the duck is roasting, prepare the hoisin sauce by combining the hoisin sauce, soy sauce, rice vinegar, honey, and sesame oil in a small bowl. Stir until well combined. Set aside.
8. Once the duck is cooked, remove it from the oven and let it rest for 10-15 minutes before carving.
9. To serve, thinly slice the roasted duck meat and skin. Place a slice of duck meat and skin onto each Chinese pancake or flour tortilla. Drizzle with hoisin sauce and top with thinly sliced green onions and cucumbers if desired.
10. Roll up the pancake or tortilla, enclosing the filling like a burrito, and serve immediately.

These Peking duck pancakes with hoisin sauce are sure to impress your wedding guests with their rich flavors and elegant presentation. Enjoy!

Smoked Trout Pâté on Crostini

Ingredients:

For the smoked trout pâté:

- 8 oz smoked trout fillets, skin removed
- 4 oz cream cheese, softened
- 2 tablespoons mayonnaise
- 1 tablespoon lemon juice
- 1 tablespoon chopped fresh dill
- 1 teaspoon Dijon mustard
- Salt and pepper to taste

For the crostini:

- Baguette or French bread, thinly sliced
- Olive oil
- Salt and pepper

Instructions:

1. Preheat your oven to 375°F (190°C). Line a baking sheet with parchment paper.
2. Prepare the crostini:
    - Arrange the thinly sliced baguette or French bread on the prepared baking sheet.
    - Brush each slice of bread with olive oil on both sides and sprinkle with salt and pepper.
    - Bake in the preheated oven for 8-10 minutes, or until golden brown and crispy. Remove from the oven and let cool.
3. Prepare the smoked trout pâté:
    - In a food processor, combine the smoked trout fillets, cream cheese, mayonnaise, lemon juice, chopped fresh dill, Dijon mustard, salt, and pepper.
    - Pulse the mixture until smooth and creamy, scraping down the sides of the food processor bowl as needed. Taste and adjust seasoning if necessary.

4. Transfer the smoked trout pâté to a serving bowl and garnish with additional chopped fresh dill if desired.
5. To serve, spread a generous amount of the smoked trout pâté onto each crostini.
6. Arrange the crostini on a serving platter and serve immediately.

These smoked trout pâté crostini are sure to impress your wedding guests with their elegant presentation and delicious flavor. Enjoy!

Miniature Beef Tacos with Guacamole and Salsa

Ingredients:

For the beef filling:

- 1 lb ground beef
- 1 tablespoon olive oil
- 1 small onion, finely chopped
- 2 cloves garlic, minced
- 1 teaspoon ground cumin
- 1 teaspoon chili powder
- 1/2 teaspoon paprika
- Salt and pepper to taste

For the guacamole:

- 2 ripe avocados
- 1 tablespoon lime juice
- 1/4 cup finely chopped red onion
- 1/4 cup chopped fresh cilantro
- Salt and pepper to taste

For the salsa:

- 1 cup diced tomatoes
- 1/4 cup finely chopped red onion
- 1/4 cup chopped fresh cilantro
- 1 tablespoon lime juice
- Salt and pepper to taste

For assembling:

- Mini taco shells or tortilla cups

- Shredded lettuce
- Shredded cheese (such as cheddar or Mexican blend)
- Sour cream (optional)
- Sliced jalapeños (optional)
- Lime wedges (for serving)

Instructions:

1. Prepare the beef filling:
   - Heat the olive oil in a skillet over medium heat. Add the chopped onion and cook until softened, about 2-3 minutes.
   - Add the minced garlic and cook for an additional 1 minute.
   - Add the ground beef to the skillet and cook, breaking it apart with a spoon, until browned and cooked through.
   - Stir in the ground cumin, chili powder, paprika, salt, and pepper. Cook for another 2-3 minutes to allow the flavors to meld. Remove from heat and set aside.
2. Prepare the guacamole:
   - Cut the avocados in half and remove the pits. Scoop the avocado flesh into a bowl and mash with a fork until smooth.
   - Stir in the lime juice, finely chopped red onion, chopped cilantro, salt, and pepper. Taste and adjust seasoning if necessary.
3. Prepare the salsa:
   - In a separate bowl, combine the diced tomatoes, finely chopped red onion, chopped cilantro, lime juice, salt, and pepper. Stir until well combined. Taste and adjust seasoning if necessary.
4. Assemble the miniature beef tacos:
   - Spoon a small amount of the beef filling into each mini taco shell or tortilla cup.
   - Top each taco with a spoonful of guacamole and salsa.
   - Garnish with shredded lettuce, shredded cheese, sour cream, sliced jalapeños, and lime wedges if desired.
5. Arrange the miniature beef tacos on a serving platter and serve immediately.

These miniature beef tacos with guacamole and salsa are sure to be a hit with your wedding guests, with their bold flavors and festive presentation. Enjoy!

Buffalo Chicken Meatballs with Blue Cheese Dip

Ingredients:

For the buffalo chicken meatballs:

- 1 lb ground chicken
- 1/2 cup breadcrumbs
- 1/4 cup finely chopped celery
- 1/4 cup finely chopped onion
- 2 cloves garlic, minced
- 1/4 cup buffalo sauce (plus more for coating)
- 1 egg
- Salt and pepper to taste
- Olive oil for greasing

For the blue cheese dip:

- 1/2 cup mayonnaise
- 1/2 cup sour cream
- 1/2 cup crumbled blue cheese
- 1 tablespoon lemon juice
- 1 clove garlic, minced
- Salt and pepper to taste
- Chopped chives or parsley for garnish (optional)

Instructions:

1. Preheat your oven to 400°F (200°C). Line a baking sheet with parchment paper and lightly grease with olive oil.
2. In a large mixing bowl, combine the ground chicken, breadcrumbs, chopped celery, chopped onion, minced garlic, buffalo sauce, egg, salt, and pepper. Mix until well combined.
3. Shape the chicken mixture into small meatballs, about 1 inch in diameter, and place them on the prepared baking sheet.

4. Bake the meatballs in the preheated oven for 15-20 minutes, or until they are cooked through and lightly browned.
5. While the meatballs are baking, prepare the blue cheese dip:
    - In a bowl, combine the mayonnaise, sour cream, crumbled blue cheese, lemon juice, minced garlic, salt, and pepper. Stir until well combined.
    - Taste and adjust seasoning if necessary. If you prefer a smoother consistency, you can blend the dip using a food processor or immersion blender.
6. Once the meatballs are cooked, remove them from the oven and let them cool for a few minutes.
7. Place the cooked meatballs in a bowl and toss them with additional buffalo sauce until they are evenly coated.
8. Arrange the buffalo chicken meatballs on a serving platter with the blue cheese dip on the side.
9. Garnish the blue cheese dip with chopped chives or parsley if desired.
10. Serve the buffalo chicken meatballs with blue cheese dip immediately, and enjoy!

These buffalo chicken meatballs with blue cheese dip are sure to be a hit at your wedding reception, with their spicy kick and creamy dip.

Teriyaki Tofu Skewers

Ingredients:

For the teriyaki marinade:

- 1/2 cup soy sauce
- 1/4 cup water
- 2 tablespoons rice vinegar
- 2 tablespoons honey or maple syrup
- 2 cloves garlic, minced
- 1 teaspoon grated ginger
- 1 tablespoon cornstarch
- 2 tablespoons water

For the tofu skewers:

- 1 block (14-16 oz) extra firm tofu, pressed and cut into cubes
- 1 bell pepper, cut into chunks
- 1 red onion, cut into chunks
- Optional: Other vegetables of your choice, such as mushrooms, zucchini, or cherry tomatoes

Instructions:

1. In a small saucepan, combine the soy sauce, water, rice vinegar, honey or maple syrup, minced garlic, and grated ginger. Bring the mixture to a simmer over medium heat.
2. In a small bowl, mix together the cornstarch and 2 tablespoons of water to create a slurry. Add the slurry to the saucepan and stir until the sauce thickens slightly. Remove from heat and let cool.
3. Once the teriyaki marinade has cooled, place the tofu cubes in a shallow dish or zip-top bag and pour the marinade over them. Make sure the tofu is evenly coated. Cover and refrigerate for at least 30 minutes, or up to 2 hours, to allow the flavors to meld.

4. While the tofu is marinating, soak wooden skewers in water for at least 30 minutes to prevent them from burning during cooking.
5. Preheat your grill or grill pan over medium-high heat. Alternatively, you can use the broiler in your oven.
6. Thread the marinated tofu cubes onto the skewers, alternating with chunks of bell pepper, red onion, and any other vegetables you're using.
7. Grill the tofu skewers for 3-4 minutes per side, or until grill marks appear and the vegetables are tender.
8. Serve the teriyaki tofu skewers hot, garnished with sesame seeds and chopped green onions if desired.

These teriyaki tofu skewers are sure to impress your wedding guests with their delicious flavor and beautiful presentation. Enjoy!

Fig and Goat Cheese Crostini with Honey Drizzle

Ingredients:

- Baguette or French bread, thinly sliced
- Olive oil
- Salt and pepper
- 4 oz goat cheese
- 6-8 fresh figs, sliced
- Honey, for drizzling
- Fresh thyme leaves, for garnish (optional)

Instructions:

1. Preheat your oven to 375°F (190°C). Line a baking sheet with parchment paper.
2. Arrange the thinly sliced baguette or French bread on the prepared baking sheet. Brush each slice of bread with olive oil on both sides and sprinkle with salt and pepper.
3. Bake the bread slices in the preheated oven for 8-10 minutes, or until golden brown and crispy. Remove from the oven and let cool slightly.
4. Spread a generous amount of goat cheese onto each toasted bread slice.
5. Top each crostini with a few slices of fresh fig.
6. Drizzle honey over the figs and goat cheese.
7. Garnish the crostini with fresh thyme leaves, if desired.
8. Arrange the fig and goat cheese crostini on a serving platter and serve immediately.

These fig and goat cheese crostini with honey drizzle are sure to impress your wedding guests with their sweet and savory flavors and elegant presentation. Enjoy!

Crab Rangoon with Sweet and Sour Sauce

Ingredients:

For the Crab Rangoon:

- 8 oz cream cheese, softened
- 1/2 cup crab meat (canned or imitation), chopped
- 2 green onions, finely chopped
- 1 clove garlic, minced
- 1 teaspoon soy sauce
- 1/2 teaspoon Worcestershire sauce
- 1/4 teaspoon ground ginger
- 24 wonton wrappers
- Vegetable oil, for frying

For the Sweet and Sour Sauce:

- 1/2 cup pineapple juice
- 1/4 cup rice vinegar
- 1/4 cup ketchup
- 2 tablespoons brown sugar
- 1 tablespoon soy sauce
- 1 teaspoon cornstarch mixed with 1 tablespoon water (optional, for thickening)

Instructions:

1. In a mixing bowl, combine the softened cream cheese, chopped crab meat, green onions, minced garlic, soy sauce, Worcestershire sauce, and ground ginger. Mix until well combined.
2. Place a small spoonful of the cream cheese mixture in the center of each wonton wrapper.
3. Moisten the edges of the wonton wrapper with water, then fold each wrapper diagonally to form a triangle. Press the edges together to seal, making sure there are no air pockets.
4. Heat vegetable oil in a deep fryer or large skillet to 350°F (175°C).

5. Carefully add the Crab Rangoon to the hot oil in batches, frying until golden brown, about 2-3 minutes per side. Remove with a slotted spoon and drain on paper towels.
6. In a small saucepan, combine the pineapple juice, rice vinegar, ketchup, brown sugar, and soy sauce for the sweet and sour sauce. Bring to a simmer over medium heat.
7. If desired, add the cornstarch-water mixture to the sauce to thicken it. Stir until the sauce has thickened slightly, then remove from heat.
8. Serve the Crab Rangoon hot with the sweet and sour sauce on the side for dipping.

These Crab Rangoon with sweet and sour sauce are sure to be a crowd-pleaser at your wedding reception, with their crispy texture and savory filling complemented by the tangy sweetness of the sauce. Enjoy!

Miniature Beef Wellingtons

Ingredients:

- 1 lb beef tenderloin fillet, trimmed and cut into 1-inch cubes
- Salt and pepper, to taste
- 2 tablespoons olive oil
- 2 tablespoons butter
- 1 small onion, finely chopped
- 2 cloves garlic, minced
- 8 oz mushrooms, finely chopped
- 2 tablespoons chopped fresh parsley
- 1 sheet puff pastry, thawed
- 1 egg, beaten (for egg wash)

Instructions:

1. Preheat your oven to 425°F (220°C).
2. Season the beef tenderloin cubes with salt and pepper.
3. Heat the olive oil in a skillet over high heat. Add the beef cubes and sear them on all sides until browned, about 1-2 minutes per side. Remove the beef from the skillet and set aside.
4. In the same skillet, melt the butter over medium heat. Add the chopped onion and garlic, and cook until softened, about 2-3 minutes.
5. Add the chopped mushrooms to the skillet and cook until they release their moisture and become golden brown, about 5-7 minutes.
6. Stir in the chopped parsley and season with salt and pepper to taste. Remove from heat and let the mushroom mixture cool slightly.
7. Roll out the puff pastry on a lightly floured surface and cut it into squares large enough to wrap around each beef cube.
8. Place a spoonful of the mushroom mixture in the center of each puff pastry square, then place a seared beef cube on top.
9. Fold the edges of the puff pastry over the beef and mushroom filling, sealing them tightly. Place the miniature Beef Wellingtons seam-side down on a baking sheet lined with parchment paper.
10. Brush the tops of the pastry with beaten egg to create a golden crust.

11. Bake the Miniature Beef Wellingtons in the preheated oven for 15-20 minutes, or until the pastry is golden brown and cooked through.
12. Remove from the oven and let the Miniature Beef Wellingtons cool slightly before serving.

These Miniature Beef Wellingtons are sure to impress your wedding guests with their tender beef, flavorful mushroom filling, and flaky pastry crust. Enjoy!

Bacon-Wrapped Jalapeño Poppers Stuffed with Cream Cheese

Ingredients:

- 12 jalapeño peppers
- 8 oz cream cheese, softened
- 1/2 cup shredded cheddar cheese
- 1/2 teaspoon garlic powder
- 1/2 teaspoon onion powder
- Salt and pepper, to taste
- 12 slices of bacon, cut in half crosswise
- Toothpicks or cocktail sticks

Instructions:

1. Preheat your oven to 375°F (190°C). Line a baking sheet with aluminum foil and place a wire rack on top.
2. Cut the jalapeño peppers in half lengthwise and remove the seeds and membranes. Use a small spoon to scrape out the seeds and white membrane, which contain most of the heat.
3. In a mixing bowl, combine the softened cream cheese, shredded cheddar cheese, garlic powder, onion powder, salt, and pepper. Mix until well combined.
4. Spoon the cream cheese mixture into each jalapeño half, filling them evenly.
5. Wrap each stuffed jalapeño half with a half slice of bacon, securing it with a toothpick or cocktail stick. Make sure the bacon covers the entire jalapeño.
6. Place the bacon-wrapped jalapeño poppers on the wire rack on the prepared baking sheet.
7. Bake in the preheated oven for 20-25 minutes, or until the bacon is crispy and the jalapeños are tender.
8. Once cooked, remove the jalapeño poppers from the oven and let them cool slightly before serving.
9. Serve the bacon-wrapped jalapeño poppers warm as an appetizer at your wedding reception.

These bacon-wrapped jalapeño poppers stuffed with cream cheese are sure to be a crowd-pleaser with their combination of spicy jalapeños, creamy cheese filling, and crispy bacon. Enjoy!

Spinach and Feta Spanakopita Triangles

Ingredients:

- 1 package (10 oz) frozen chopped spinach, thawed and squeezed dry
- 1 cup crumbled feta cheese
- 1/4 cup grated Parmesan cheese
- 2 green onions, finely chopped
- 2 cloves garlic, minced
- 1/4 teaspoon dried dill
- Salt and pepper, to taste
- 1/4 cup olive oil, plus more for brushing
- 12 sheets phyllo dough, thawed according to package instructions
- Melted butter or olive oil spray (optional, for brushing)

Instructions:

1. Preheat your oven to 375°F (190°C). Line a baking sheet with parchment paper.
2. In a large mixing bowl, combine the chopped spinach, crumbled feta cheese, grated Parmesan cheese, chopped green onions, minced garlic, dried dill, salt, pepper, and 1/4 cup of olive oil. Mix until well combined.
3. Place one sheet of phyllo dough on a clean work surface and brush it lightly with olive oil. Place another sheet of phyllo dough on top and brush with olive oil again. Repeat with two more sheets of phyllo dough, brushing each layer with olive oil.
4. Cut the stacked phyllo dough sheets lengthwise into 3 equal strips.
5. Place a spoonful of the spinach and feta mixture at the bottom of each strip of phyllo dough.
6. Fold one corner of the phyllo dough over the filling to form a triangle, then continue folding the triangle onto itself, as you would fold a flag, until you reach the end of the strip. Repeat with the remaining phyllo dough and filling.
7. Place the spanakopita triangles on the prepared baking sheet and brush the tops lightly with melted butter or olive oil spray, if desired.
8. Bake in the preheated oven for 20-25 minutes, or until the spanakopita triangles are golden brown and crispy.
9. Remove from the oven and let cool slightly before serving.

10. Serve the spinach and feta spanakopita triangles warm as an appetizer at your wedding reception.

These spinach and feta spanakopita triangles are sure to be a hit with their flaky phyllo dough crust and flavorful spinach and cheese filling. Enjoy!